The Adventures

No Kiss-No Hug

Written by:
Gin Noon Spaulding

Illustrated by:
ePublishing eXperts

The Adventures of LiLi Series

Book 1 - A Miracle at Bates Memorial
Book 2 - Picture Perfect - NOT
Book 3 - Jump-O-Ween
Book 4 - No Kiss-No Hug

Order books on Amazon, Goodreads, or on Mrs. Spaulding's website (www.ginnoonspaulding.com).

No Kiss-No Hug

Published by Author Academy Elite

P.O. Box 43

Powell, OH 43065

Illustrator: ePublishingeXperts

Library of Congress Control Number: 2020916336

ISBN: 978-1-64746-468-4 (Paperback)

ISBN: 978-1-64746-469-1 (Hardback)

ISBN: 978-1-64746-470-7 (Ebook)

theadventuresoflili2003@gmail.com
www.ginnoonspaulding.com

P.O. Box 91967
Louisville, KY 40291

Dedication

I'd like to dedicate this book to all of my family, especially my parents Leonard and Lisa Noon. They were wonderful, caring, loving parents who always encouraged me to try my best and to remember that I was just as good as anybody else. My daddy was the hardest worker EVER, and even though he was harassed on his factory job for being a Black man, he never complained. He had a quiet strength and continued to work, until he retired. My mama was a fighter and a champion for the underprivileged and the forgotten. She would help anyone in need. I still remember my mama feeding the neighborhood children and strangers who came to our door, trying to sell goods. My parents were opposites in many ways, but they agreed on one thing...their love for me and my siblings.

Like my mama, I volunteer to help others, especially the homeless. Like my daddy, I am a hardworker, and I always try to do my best. I'm grateful to God for the values my parents instilled in me.

I'd like to thank my family, sorors, and close friends for supporting me through my faith walk in writing books about our Li-Li. I'd like to really thank my sister, Jan Noon Perkins, for helping me understand my daughter better, since the two of them are so much alike!

Gin Noon Spaulding - M.Ed

Foreword

Sensory processing differences are likely to impact how a child interacts and communicates with others. In her newest release, Gin Noon Spaulding describes an uncomfortable but common situation that children with sensory processing differences often face.

As a licensed Speech Language Pathologist, I had the opportunity to meet Gin and her family when her daughter, Maleah, was referred to me through Kentucky's Early Intervention Program. Maleah's initial referral was just for expressive language, a concern that she wasn't saying words, yet we quickly realized she was experiencing sensory processing differences. I had the opportunity to educate and guide her family in the process of learning more about sensory processing and how it affects communication.

I have watched throughout the years as Gin has advocated for her daughter. She has sought out wonderful programs, schools and resources to allow her daughter to achieve her full potential. I'm so proud that I've had the pleasure to watch Maleah grow into a young woman who is beginning her Senior year at one of the top high schools in Kentucky.. Maleah is fierce and ready to take on the world.

Gin is now bringing awareness and education to you, her readers, and to all the children you share this book with. Let's go on another adventure as Gin beautifully illustrates Li-Li's desire for No Kiss, No Hug.

-Dana Moutachouik, M.Ed, CCC-SLP

Hey… It is me, again… Maleah!
You can still just call me Li-Li.

Guess where I am going today?
Go on…. guess!

No… it is NOT China

No… it is NOT France

No… it is NOT the library

No… it is NOT to Kentucky Kingdom, even though I wouldn't mind going there! It IS my favorite amusement park.

Do you give up? Well, I will tell you. I am going to see my MeMa and Pops in Tennessee. They are my mommy's mommy and daddy! We try to see them at least every three months or so. My mommy wishes we lived closer to them, and I do, too.

My Pops is soooo funny. He gives me rides on his back and always has time for me. He listens to me, and when we go to Tullahoma, he makes me Pops Fries! They are THE BEST FRIES EVER!

My MeMa loves me! She likes to read and talk to me. I like going to church, McDonald's, and anywhere fun with her! My favorite thing to do is swinging in their big, front yard swing. Sometimes, I get to sing and play with the other children at church, with my cousins, or in my mommy's old neighborhood.
We always have the BEST time, but…

There is one thing I really don't like. That's the kisses and hugs my grandparents want to give me. I just don't like hugs and kisses. My mommy says I'm just like my Auntie Jan. She didn't like hugs and kisses either.

My mommy asked me to just let Mema
and Pops hug and kiss me, since they don't
see me that much. I said yes, but I can
NOT take the kiss. NO WAY!
Just the thought of all that hugging and
kissing makes me want to have a….

LETDOWN!!!

We ride and ride and ride some more, all the way to Tullahoma, TN. I don't mind riding for like... FOREVER because I get to watch Dora and Baby Einstein videos, read books, sing with my Dora CD, and sleep the whole time.

My mommy, daddy, and grandparents start talking about me, Louisville, Tullahoma, the people, and our Tennessee family, when the front door opens. It's my favorite cousins… Cousin Monica and her daughter, Sadiyyah, who is just a year older than me. I let Cousin Monica hug me, since she never tries to kiss me. I also hug Sadiyyah, and we play with her new toy.

I love my family, and I am so glad they understand me. Now, whenever I go back to Tullahoma to visit, my grandparents always hug me and say, "NO KISS!" Then, we all laugh and laugh!!

THE END

We always stop to use the restroom, and sometimes my mommy and daddy buy traveling chips (potato chips) for me. I don't get to eat them often, so I really like eating them in the truck, while doing many of my favorite things! But… I'm still thinking about MeMa and Pops trying to hug and kiss me. Yuck!

At last… we make it to Tullahoma, TN! When we pass the Wal-Mart, my belly starts to get butterflies, just thinking about all the hugging and possible kissing. As we pull into the driveway, I see my MeMa and Pops standing on the front porch, waving at us. I am so happy to see them, but… the butterflies are getting stronger and stronger.

I unbuckle my seatbelt and wait for my daddy to help me get out of the car, since we have a child safety thingy. He helps me get out, and I run to see my grandparents. I let them hug me, but I just CAN'T take the kiss. I put my hand up and say, "No KISS!"

My grandparents just laugh and laugh. My mommy says, "You know that Maleah has sensory issues to touch. She really doesn't like hugs, and she especially doesn't like kisses. But... she really loves you and has made an exception for you, right Li-Li?" I say, "Yes!" Then, I put my hand up again and say... "NO KISS!!" Everybody laughs and laughs, and then we go into the house.

Signs Of Tactile Dysfunction (https://www.sensory-processing-disorder.com/sensory-processing-disorder-checklist.html)

1. Hypersensitivity To Touch (Tactile Defensiveness)
— becomes fearful, anxious or aggressive with light or unexpected touch
— as an infant, did/does not like to be held or cuddled; may arch back, cry, and pull away
— distressed when diaper is being, or needs to be, changed
— appears fearful of, or avoids standing in close proximity to other people or peers (especially in lines)
— becomes frightened when touched from behind or by someone/something they can not see (such as under a blanket)
— complains about having hair brushed; may be very picky about using a particular brush
— bothered by rough bed sheets (i.e., if old and bumpy)
— avoids group situations for fear of the unexpected touch
— resists friendly or affectionate touch from anyone besides parents or siblings (and sometimes them too!)
— dislikes kisses, will wipe off place where kissed
— prefers hugs
— a raindrop, water from the shower, or wind blowing on the skin may feel like torture and produce adverse and avoidance reactions
— may overreact to minor cuts, scrapes, and or bug bites
— avoids touching certain textures of material (blankets, rugs, stuffed animals)
— refuses to wear new or stiff clothes, clothes with rough textures, turtlenecks, jeans, hats, or belts, etc.
— avoids using hands for play
— avoids/dislikes/aversive to messy play;, i.e., sand, mud, water, glue, glitter, playdoh, slime, shaving cream/funny foam etc.
— will be distressed by dirty hands and want to wipe or wash them frequently
— excessively ticklish
— distressed by seams in socks and may refuse to wear them
— distressed by clothes rubbing on skin; may want to wear shorts and short sleeves year round, toddlers may prefer to be naked and pull diapers and clothes off constantly
— or, may want to wear long sleeve shirts and long pants year round to avoid having skin exposed
— distressed about having face washed

— distressed about having hair, toenails, or fingernails cut
— resists brushing teeth and is extremely fearful of the dentist
— is a picky eater, only eating certain tastes and textures; mixed textures tend to be avoided as well as hot or cold foods; resists trying new foods
— may refuse to walk barefoot on grass or sand
— may walk on toes only

2. Hyposensitivity To Touch (Under-Responsive):
— may crave touch, needs to touch everything and everyone
— is not aware of being touched/bumped unless done with extreme force or intensity
— is not bothered by injuries, like cuts and bruises, and shows no distress with shots (may even say they love getting shots!)
— may not be aware that hands or face are dirty or feel his/her nose running
— may be self-abusive; pinching, biting, or banging his own head
— mouths objects excessively
— frequently hurts other children or pets while playing
— repeatedly touches surfaces or objects that are soothing (i.e., blanket)
— seeks out surfaces and textures that provide strong tactile feedback
— thoroughly enjoys and seeks out messy play
— craves vibrating or strong sensory input
— has a preference and craving for excessively spicy, sweet, sour, or salty foods

3. Poor Tactile Perception And Discrimination:
— has difficulty with fine motor tasks such as buttoning, zipping, and fastening clothes
— may not be able to identify which part of their body was touched if they were not looking
— may be afraid of the dark
— may be a messy dresser; looks disheveled, does not notice pants are twisted, shirt is half untucked, shoes are untied, one pant leg is up and one is down, etc.
— has difficulty using scissors, crayons, or silverware
— continues to mouth objects to explore them even after age two
— has difficulty figuring out physical characteristics of objects; shape, size, texture, temperature, weight, etc.
— may not be able to identify objects by feel, uses vision to help; such as, reaching into backpack or desk to retrieve an item.

A SPECIAL note from the Author:

Thank you, thank you for reading No Kiss-No Hug, my fourth book in the children's series, The Adventures of Li-Li! I hope you enjoyed reading it, as much as I enjoyed writing it, just for you... my friends.

All of the books in The Adventures of Li-Li series are about Li-Li and various sensory issues. A Miracle at Bates Memorial is my first book, which is an introduction to sensory issues, Li-Li, and our family. Book two, Picture Perfect- NOT, is about visual sensory issues, Jump-O-Ween (Book 3) is about proprioceptive (body awareness) sensory issues, and No Kiss-No Hug (Book 4) is about Tactile Dysfunction (sensory issues to touch).

I am available for parent talks, author's visits, events, workshops, conferences, health fairs, etc. Please visit my website: www.ginnoonspaulding, Facebook page www.Facebook.com/gustgin/, Twitter - @gustgin, and Instagram - @gustgin9807

As there are 7 sensory issues, I plan to write at least eight books in... one for each sensory issue and the introductory book.

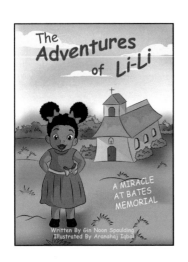

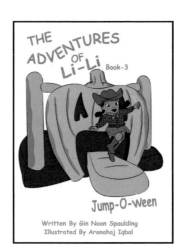

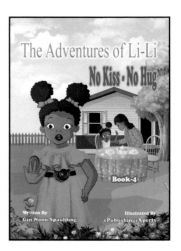

The Adventures of LiLi Series